THE TWELVE DAYS OF
CHRISTMAS

ALISON JAY

templar publishing

On the first
day of Christmas
my true love gave to me...

a partridge in a pear tree.

On the second day of Christmas my true love gave to me...

two turtle doves
and a partridge in a pear tree.

*

On the third day of Christmas my true love gave to me...

three French hens,
two turtle doves
and a partridge in a pear tree.

On the fourth day of Christmas my true love gave to me...

four calling birds,
three French hens,
two turtle doves
and a partridge in a pear tree.

*

On the fifth day of Christmas my true love gave to me...

five gold rings

four calling birds,
three French hens,
two turtle doves
and a partridge in a pear tree.

*

On the sixth day of Christmas
my true love gave to me...

six geese-a-laying,
five gold rings,
four calling birds,
three French hens,
two turtle doves
and a partridge in a pear tree.

On the seventh day of Christmas my true love gave to me...

seven swans-a-swimming,
six geese-a-laying,
five gold rings,
four calling birds,
three French hens,
two turtle doves
and a partridge in a pear tree.

*

On the eighth day of Christmas
my true love gave to me...

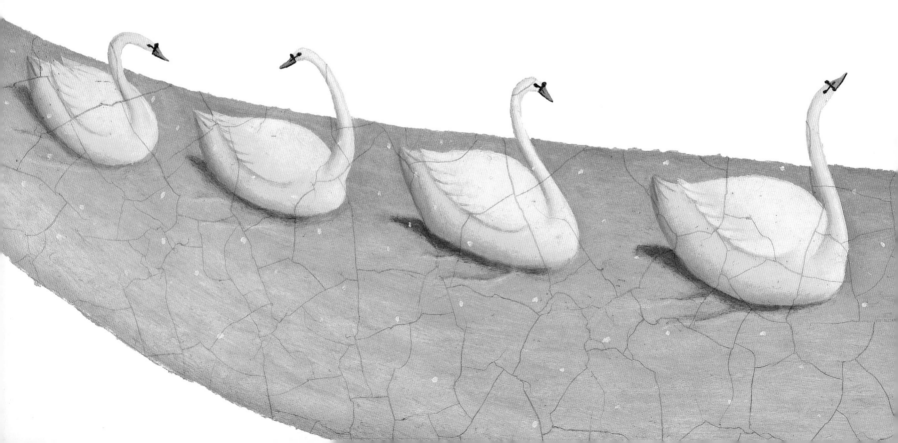

eight maids-a-milking,
seven swans-a-swimming,
six geese-a-laying,
five gold rings,
four calling birds,
three French hens,
two turtle doves
and a partridge in a pear tree.

On the ninth day of Christmas my true love gave to me...

nine drummers drumming,
eight maids-a-milking,
seven swans-a-swimming,
six geese-a-laying,
five gold rings,
four calling birds,
three French hens,
two turtle doves
and a partridge in a pear tree.

On the tenth day of Christmas
my true love gave to me...

ten ladies dancing,
nine drummers drumming,
eight maids-a-milking,
seven swans-a-swimming,
six geese-a-laying,
five gold rings,
four calling birds,
three French hens,
two turtle doves
and a partridge in a pear tree.

On the eleventh day of
Christmas my true love gave to me...

eleven pipers piping,
ten ladies dancing,
nine drummers drumming,
eight maids-a-milking,
seven swans-a-swimming,
six geese-a-laying,
five gold rings,
four calling birds,
three French hens,
two turtle doves
and a partridge in a pear tree.

On the twelfth day of Christmas my true love gave to me...

twelve lords-a-leaping, eleven pipers piping, ten ladies dancing,

nine drummers drumming, eight maids-a-milking,

four calling birds, three French hens, two turtle doves…

seven swans-a-swimming, six geese-a-laying, five gold rings,

and a partridge
in a pear tree.

For leaping-lord Simon, love from the dancing goose – A. J.

A TEMPLAR BOOK

First published in the UK in 2014 by Templar Publishing,
an imprint of The Templar Company Limited,
Deepdene Lodge, Deepdene Avenue, Dorking, Surrey, RH5 4AT, UK
www.templarco.co.uk

First edition

ISBN 978-1-84877-913-6

Designed by janie louise hunt

Printed in China